Fishing Flies

Fishing Flies

A practical guide to the craft of fly tying

Martin Ford

LORENZ BOOKS

First published in 1999 by Lorenz Books

Lorenz Books is an imprint of
Anness Publishing Limited
Hermes House
88-89 Blackfriars Road
London SE1 8HA

Published in the USA by Lorenz Books
Anness Publishing Inc.
27 West 20th Street
New York, NY 10011
(800) 354-9657

This edition distributed in Canada by
Raincoast Books
8680 Cambie Street
Vancouver, British Columbia V6P 6M9

A CIP catalogue record for this book is available from the British Library

ISBN 1 85967 890 4

Publisher Joanna Lorenz
Editor Simona Hill
Designer Simon Wilder
Photographer Susan Ford
Illustrators Mike Atkinson and Penny Brown
Editorial Reader Hayley Kerr
Production Controller Joanna King

Printed and bound in Singapore

10 9 8 7 6 5 4 3 2 1

This book is for Catrina, Matthew and Lucy.

I would like to extend my sincere thanks to my sister Susan Ford for her
superb photography skills and patience and to Andrew Flitcroft for tying the
carefully crafted flies featured in the step-by-step sequences.

Thanks also to Philip White of Lathkill Tackle, Derbyshire, England, for
his help and time in sourcing materials used in this book; to Turrall & Co,
Devon, England, for their assistance in providing the ready-tied examples of
flies shown in these pages and also to the House of Hardy Museum,
Northumberland, Scotland.

CONTENTS

ℐNTRODUCTION

ℌS THE ANGLER'S FLY LINE glides silently out across the water, the fire-red sun sinks slowly down behind the hills, heralding the demise of the day. The silhouette of the neatly tied dry fly sits motionless and undisturbed on the surface film of the tranquil water.

In the distance a single church bell begins its hallowed toll, echoing out across the valley. Far out over the water, the distant crashing of trout can be heard as they begin their dusk patrol. Standing alone in the half light, the angler waits, rod in hand, at the ready … waiting for a trout to be deceived by the imitation of nature that has been so carefully created. An aggressive swirl on the water a few yards behind the buoyant fly alerts the angler that the quarry is now near. Suddenly, without warning, the dry fly is engulfed and torn from the surface into the depths below. The line tightens, and contact is made between hunter and hunted.

The hooked trout breaks through the surface and embarks on an aerobatic display in a bid to rid itself of the deceiving fly. The fight is over, and in the dying light of day a silver-speckled rainbow trout is drawn to the waiting net. Quickly dispatched with the aid of a priest, the angler's prize lies still and motionless on the soft, dew-soaked grass, glistening like a diamond under the light of the newly risen moon.

To study closely the creatures on which the game fish feeds and to become a master imitator with both feather and fur at the vice are, when combined with the gentle art of casting a fly line, the purest of ingredients for successful fly fishing.

6

GONE FISHING

THROUGHOUT HISTORY MAN HAS HUNTED to survive. While fishing may no longer be an act of necessity for many, it has developed to become one of the most popular sports in the world. Fly fishing in particular, once a sport for the gentry, still has a reputation for exclusivity and prestige.

Fly fishing is a skilful art, one where man can pit his wits against nature, and at the same time, be at one with the world around him. Though the techniques can be learnt, most anglers spend a lifetime perfecting and mastering the skills; learning how to read the water, how to understand the quarry and knowing when to strike. The fascination lies in the mystery, the anticipation and the opportunity to outwit the fish with a man-made creation. Every fishing expedition is different, offering a continual learning opportunity. Since the environment changes hour by hour, the flies that catch the choicest fish on one occasion may not at the next.

Equipment and clothing has evolved, too, as innovative manufacturers introduce the latest materials to sustain the market. New styles and methods of fishing produce new equipment. The once-popular cane rods, though still in use, have been superseded with high-tech tackle made of space-age precision-tooled materials. While this new lightweight equipment may be more pleasant to use, it is still the angler's skill that determines the success or failure of a day's fly fishing.

SALMON

Salmosalar

OF ALL THE VARIOUS *Salmonidae*, the Atlantic salmon is the largest. It is found in many of the river systems that border the North Atlantic Sea. From Canada to Russia and Scotland, the salmon is highly prized by the game angler for its sporting fight. Its cousin, the Pacific salmon, can be found in rivers across North America.

There is often much confusion in the identification of young salmon and trout. The salmon can be distinguished by the greater number of larger cycloid scales running along its lateral line – as many as 130 in all. The trout has far fewer, and they are much smaller in size. Salmon have an amazing life cycle and live a remarkable double life. The adult salmon spends most of its life at sea, but when ready to reproduce, it embarks on an epic journey back to freshwater, to the same river where it was born. Salmon travel in their thousands to search out their place of birth and spawn, to ensure the future of their species.

The sea is where the salmon grows by feeding freely on all species of shrimp and other marine creatures. However, once the urge to spawn is triggered and the salmon returns to freshwater, it will not feed for the duration of its stay in the river. When fresh run from the sea (for Pacific salmon, this is mid- to late summer), both the female and the male are of a similar colour. The male, or cock salmon, has a pronounced lower jaw called a hook or kype. This in time becomes upturned. The skull of the male is also rather elongated in comparison to the female. As the Atlantic salmon forge their way up-river from autumn onward to return to the redds (small depressions sculpted from the gravel river bed by the hen salmon) to spawn, a distinct change in skin coloration occurs in both the cock and the hen salmon. The cock begins to lose his coat of silver.

This is replaced by a pinkish-red covering, speckled with scarlet spots, over a marbled, purple and brown back. These are his last days of grandeur as, following spawning, the male will die. The hen salmon also takes on spawning colours, but hers are not as grand as those of the male. Small pinkish spots form on the upper body and the skin transforms to a smoky-grey, brushed with a blue sheen. She also develops a small kype.

Once the ritual of egg laying is over, any surviving females (many of them will also perish) will once more return to a silver colour and set a course back to the sea. At this stage of their incredible journey these spent females are referred to as kelts. The eggs on the spawning grounds will gradually develop from fry into infant salmon, called parr. During this stage of their development they resemble small trout, with a similar brown spotted coat. They remain in the sanctuary of freshwater for a minimum of one year. In some cases it can be up to six years before the sea beckons to them. When they slowly drop back down-river towards the estuary, the salmon parr become smolts as they make the gradual change from fresh to salt water. Some will return to the river of their birth after only one year at sea.

The amount of time salmon spend feeding at sea dictates their growth rate. The salmon that do return are referred to as grilse or springers and weigh anything up to 2.75kg (6lb). It is at this stage of their lives that they are most vulnerable to capture and are a much sought-after quarry. The current British rod-caught record for the salmon still stands at 28.8kg (64lb) for a fine specimen caught from River Tay in Scotland on 7 October 1922. The monster fish, which had attained a length of 1.4m (54in), was caught by Georgina Ballantine.

BROOK TROUT

Salvelinus fontinalis

THE AMERICAN BROOK TROUT is a species of char, originating from North America. It is often caught in rivers that flow out into the Atlantic. The brook trout is well distributed across Europe and is to be found in other parts of the world such as southern Africa and Asia. It was introduced into the British Isles in 1868 but has only recently gained in popularity with British anglers and trout fishery owners.

With its highly colourful, patterned body, it is a handsome, striking species and a hard-fighting fish once hooked on a fly. It can be distinguished from other species of trout by a series of dark wavy lines (vermiculations), which form a marbled pattern across its back and upper fins. It also has a thicker-set appearance than its near relation, the brown trout. Its green-brown back is speckled with an array of red, blue, cream and yellow spots. On the underside of the body, the brook trout has orange-red fins and a pinkish-cream belly. An adult has a well-developed set of upper and lower teeth. The dorsal fin has approximately 12–14 major rays, and the pelvic fin has between eight and ten.

In the wild, brook trout spawn during late summer and early autumn. The fry hatch from the eggs after 100 days but take three years to reach sexual maturity. Their life span is just six years. The average weight of the brook trout is around 900g (2lb). However, in North America individual specimens have been caught on rod and line weighing upward of 5.5kg (12lb).

SEA TROUT

Salmo trutta trutta

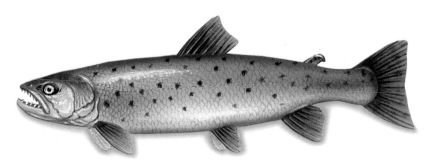

OFTEN REFERRED TO AS A "BAR OF SILVER", the sea trout is a form of sea-going brown trout. The difference is that the sea trout has migratory habits and returns to the sea. Conceived in freshwater, the sea trout shares many of the brown trout's characteristics prior to migration; it eats the same food and lives in the same water. Like the salmon, the sea trout goes through several changes throughout its early life. At birth it is referred to as an alevin, progressing to a fry and becoming a parr. As a parr, the sea trout ventures further from its birthplace to explore the river. After three years, its coat of mottled brown develops a silver appearance, a camouflage to protect it from other sea-going predators. Now regarded as smolts, they move in large shoals downstream towards the estuary. This mass exodus from the river usually occurs in spring.

At sea, new sources of food are sampled and the sea trout must become wise to the many enemies it now has. Many smolts return to the river in early autumn, having grown to a weight of 225g (8oz) or more and measuring 30cm (12in) in length. These fish, now called "finnock" or "whitling", never grow to a great size, and so it is the sea trout that have stayed at sea for two or more years before returning to spawn that are the target of the fly fisher. These fish can reach weights close to 3.6–4.5kg (8–10lbs). Once the sea trout has spawned, it is known as a kelt until the time when it travels downstream to repeat the process.

RAINBOW TROUT

Oncorhynchus mykiss

A NATIVE OF THE NORTH American Pacific coast, the brightly coloured rainbow trout can be found in the clear lush waters of the Rocky Mountain streams and rivers. Rainbow trout are well distributed throughout the world and are a major sporting fish of the British Isles. They were first introduced into English waters in 1884 and later taken to Ireland and Scotland.

Rainbow trout bear a slight resemblance to the sea trout. There are several varieties of rainbow, including the much famed American steelhead trout. Steelheads, like sea trout, migrate to the sea after spawning. Today, many thousands of rainbow trout are farm-reared for introduction to stillwaters and reservoir fisheries, and are commonly known as "stockies" or "stockers". They are highly regarded for their food value. When cooked, the flesh is a light shade of pink.

Like the brown trout, the rainbow has a liberal splattering of spots along the upper half of the body. However, this is where the similarity ends. The spots on a rainbow are black in colour, unlike those of the brown trout. The underside of the rainbow trout's body, extending to the flanks, is light silver smothered in a crimson-pink sheen. Running parallel with the lateral line on each flank is a reddish-pink band. This is known as the rainbow and is very prominent on a freshly caught fish. The scales of the rainbow trout are small and neat. It has 10–12 rays in the dorsal fin and as many as 17 in the pectoral fin. Both upper and lower jaws have fine strong teeth.

Rainbow trout feed freely on a variety of water insects and are easily fooled by the angler's imitation fly. Artificially reared rainbow trout are not able to spawn in a natural state as they are bred in captivity. In a few isolated instances where several rainbow trout have escaped from man-made fisheries, they have tried to set up colonies in some of the river systems.

In their native waters of North America, rainbow trout spawn between April and June. In the British Isles they also spawn in the winter from late December through to the following April. The few natural spawnings that do take place do so in early spring as the water temperature begins to rise.

On reaching sexual maturity, the male rainbow trout differs from the female in appearance. The head becomes slightly elongated, and the back and shoulders darken in colour to show the much more prominent rainbow marking along the flanks. It is possible to gauge the age of a rainbow trout from scale readings. These readings indicate that rainbows in general have a short life span of four to five years.

In the clear flowing waters of the American Rocky Mountains, the rainbow trout runs wild and is a prime target for the sport fisher. Rainbow trout are essential to the British fly fisher too. Many thousands are caught each season from the growing numbers of commercial fisheries. Unlike the stocked or wild brown trout of British waters, the rainbow trout is a fairly easy species to catch on the fly. In many fisheries it is the policy to replace tomorrow what was caught today, ensuring a never-ending supply of sport. Worldwide, it is becoming common practice to promote a catch-and-release policy. This will help ensure the survival of the wild fish despite their inability to breed in great numbers in the British Isles. The future of the species remains bright.

BROWN TROUT

Salmo trutta

WIDELY DISTRIBUTED ACROSS THE WORLD from Norway to North Africa, the brown trout thrives in crystal clear, clean water, where it feeds on all manner of insect life. From an early age, brown trout feed freely on the fry of other species, but it is the older and larger fish that rely on other species for their main diet. These large brown trout are referred to as cannibal trout.

In small rivers and brooks the brown trout rarely exceeds 450g (1lb) in weight. In larger reservoirs and stillwaters, it may weigh 2.75–5.5kg (6–12lb). Bigger specimens have been found, including a giant of over 22.5kg (50lb) trapped when a lake in Yugoslavia was drained.

Brown trout are easy to identify. Generally they have a brownish upper body, which is speckled with red and black spots circled with dark or cream halos. Variations in the main body colour occurs depending on the environment in which they live. The underside of the body is pale cream or yellow, with orange, blemished fins. The scales covering the body are small and compact, and the dorsal fin has a minimum of 12 rays. Like the salmon, the male brown trout develops a kype at the end of the lower jaw. Bigger, older males may have a large head which looks out of proportion with the slim body behind it. Spawning takes place from autumn to winter but varies depending on the water temperature. The fry emerge from the yolk sac in the spring of the following year, and within days they disperse from the spawning site.

GRAYLING

Thymallus thymallus

OF THE SIX SPECIES OF GRAYLING that are derived from the genus *Thymallus*, two are of interest to the fly fisher – the European and the Arctic grayling. The Arctic grayling is located as far north as Siberia.

This much-treasured sport fish is aptly named the "lady of the stream" because of its gracious appearance. The grayling has a spectacular, large, colourful dorsal fin which it uses like a rudder in fast-flowing currents. The fin has as many as seven spiny rays and up to 24 long branched rays, and is usually larger in the male of the species. When the fish is ready to spawn, the fin is tinged with a radiant purple film coated in reddish-black spots – thought to be a signalling device to an interested mate. The fin may also have a fine red rim prior to spawning. When hooked, the grayling uses the colossal fin to help slip the angler's hook.

The scales on a grayling are large and present all over the dull silvery body down to the neck of the tail. The head is pointed and the pupils are blue. Its mouth is small and slightly underslung, a benefit for this bottom-feeding species.

Spawning usually takes place in spring. Depending on her size, the female will lay between 600 and 10,000 eggs, which are susceptible to attack from all species. For those grayling fry that do hatch, it is another three years before they reach maturity and are able to repeat the spawning process. A mature grayling is around 450g (1lb) in weight. The average life span is between six and nine years.

RIVER FISHING FOR
SALMON

FOR MANY KEEN ANGLERS, the ultimate in fly fishing is to battle with the king of the river, the mighty salmon. Stout tackle in the form of a 5m (15ft) fly rod and a heavy line are just two requirements for the pursuit of this powerful species. Another is a strong leader to which a fly is attached and cast up and across the river. The line travels in an arc-like manner, swinging down, across and into the flow. As the line moves around, the fly is drawn behind, searching out the water and covering the lay of the salmon. It is common practice to make several casts with the fly in order to cover every area of the water before moving on to try in a different spot. A deep pool at the end of a shallow run will often be the resting place of a freshly run salmon as it rests on its journey up-river. Let the water's flow work the fly – it is the skill of the search that brings the reward when the fly is taken in a moment of aggression by the salmon. Once hooked, this species has the power to strip a fly reel down to the backing as it begins a series of heart-wrenching downstream runs.

Above: *Loch Garry in Scotland.*
Right: *The battle is won and a prime salmon comes to the net.*

RIVER FISHING FOR
SEA TROUT

ONE OF THE BEST TIMES TO FISH FOR SEA TROUT on the river is at night when the fly fisher has the upper hand. Provided the approach is quiet, the sea trout will not be aware of any presence.

To gain the best geographical view of a sea trout lair, spend time on the bank during daylight prior to fishing. This enables the fly fisher to map out any unforeseen obstacles. A stout, single-handed fly rod of 3m (10ft) matched with a sink-tip line of an 8–9 rating should suffice for most occasions. Leader strength needs to be of a minimum 4.5kg (10lb) breaking strain to ensure the safe landing of a hard-fighting sea trout. Flies are a matter of personal choice and different waters will have their own established patterns. Carry a good selection of the more popular patterns, such as the Mallard and Claret, Peter Ross, and Teal Blue and Silver. Small tubes, flies and waddingtons are worth a try if the fish are lying in deeper water.

If the moon sheds enough light, you may fancy indulging in the sport of fishing the Wake fly. This is a method that works extremely well in shallow water where sea trout can be seen swirling at flies on the surface. The Wake fly is constructed from highly buoyant deer hair and resembles a miniature hedgehog. Using a floating line with a 2.9m (9½ft) leader, the fly is cast down and across the river and is then retrieved with a series of short, sharp pulls. When worked in this manner, a small wake is caused by the disturbance of water rippling behind the fly. Once sighted, the sea trout usually stalks it, taking it from behind with a swirl as it engulfs the fly and is hooked.

Above: *A fresh sea trout fooled by the fly.*

Left: *Fishing on the banks of a river in Norway.*

RIVER FISHING FOR
WILD BROWN TROUT

WHEN IN PURSUIT OF WILD BROWN TROUT on small rivers or streams, caution is the key to outwitting your quarry. Before attempting to cast a line, walk the beat and observe the habit of the flow, looking for the lie of the trout you seek. Survey the water carefully and study the clean gravel bottom when looking for your quarry.

The last few hours of day are often the best time to take to the river in search of the wild brown trout, for this is when they will be busily engrossed in feeding on the feast of the evening hatch. Spinners and duns are plentiful as they fall to the surface of the water, providing a food-rich table for the trout. Travelling light, armed with a rod, line and a selection of flies, you will be able to cover a wide area before the day is done. Look for signs of insect life over the water and observe the surface for activity from rising fish. On the clear shallow waters, arm yourself with a floating line and a long cast of clear monofilament so as not to draw attention from the trout. Present a dry fly slightly upstream of the trout so that the fly tantalizingly drifts within his field of vision. Be ready to take command as he rises from his station to intercept and sip in the fly. Once hooked, he is a hardy fighter and will give great sport for such a little fellow, darting and diving in the clear, running water.

Above: *A wild brown trout displays its full colour.*

Right: *Travelling light and fishing on the move will enable the angler to cover more water.*

RIVER FISHING FOR
GRAYLING

SEEK OUT THE GRAYLING in the swift oxygen-rich waters of small rivers and streams. Holding fast in the running water, using her giant fin as a rudder, the grayling will be searching the river bed for small shrimp on which to dine. To succeed in catching one of this most splendid species requires the angler to fish a pattern of fly beneath the fast-flowing water. Specially tied, weighted bugs and nymphs are often the pattern used to outwit the grayling. Look for a fast run of water and the grayling will be sitting in wait at the end of the run tasting the morsels of food travelling in the stream.

A light tackle approach will give the best sport from this hard-fighting species. A 2.1m (7ft) fly rod matched with a small reel and loaded with a four floating line coupled to a light leader is a well-balanced match for the angler fishing for grayling. Cast your chosen fly into the fast water and allow the current to make the fly work. At the end of the run where fast water meets smooth, twitch the fly back to the rod in slow jerky movements. When the grayling strikes, she will exert an explosion of power in the first frantic run. Be ready to yield line and play out the lady carefully, but with authority. If she heads for the deeper water you have a spirited fight on your hands, and every ounce of energy she possesses will be used in a bid to rid the hook. She will kite in the flow, using the giant fin as a rudder.

Above: *A bold fighter, the lady of the stream lies defeated.*

RESERVOIR FISHING FOR
Rainbow Trout

PPLY BOTH FLOATING LINE AND SINKING LINE TACTICS to catching reservoir rainbow trout. Whether fishing from the bank or a boat, the fly fisher has a wide choice of fly patterns to choose from. The standard choice for reservoir fishing is a 2.9m (9½ft) rod with a line rating of 7–8. A medium-sized fly reel is employed to hold the line, which should be fitted with a long monofilament leader of 2.75–3.5kg (6–8lb) breaking strain. As the bank fly fisher knows, at dawn and dusk the rainbow trout will be patrolling the margins searching out the natural casualties, blown on to the water from the bankside vegetation.

At the peak of the day many of the rainbows will move out from the bank to feed. This is when the angler in search of sport is advised to take to a boat and fish on the drift. Look carefully at the surface of the water and you will see wind lanes that carry a rich supply of food to the trout. Make your choice of fly pattern carefully and try to match the natural food the trout are feeding on. A small Pheasant Tail Nymph is a good choice to try in these conditions. Surface-feeding rainbows ignoring a small fly pattern can sometimes be caught when fishing a cast fitted with two flies, one of these being fished on a dropper. Choose a muddler for the dropper fly since this is used purely for attraction, and use a Silver Invicta for the point fly. Cast the flies upwind of a rising rainbow and begin to strip the line back to the rod in a fast manner. This will cause the muddler to create a surface wake as it is drawn through the water. The inquisitive rainbow will often rise, following the muddler, and eventually fall to the Silver Invicta.

Above: *A freshly caught rainbow trout fooled by the fly.*

Left: *Fishing from a boat on a reservoir will help you cover more water.*

RESERVOIR FISHING FOR
BROWN TROUT

LIKE THE RAINBOW TROUT, the stocked brown trout of the reservoir can be pursued from either the bank or a boat. However, brown trout are more cunning and, although caught on attractor patterns, it is the angler who can match the hatch who often catches the better quality brown trout.

Tackle required for the brown trout is similar to that used for fishing rainbow trout. Fishing in sheltered bays at the end of the day, the angler may often hit upon a rising brown trout with a carefully cast dry fly. A Black and Peacock Spider is just one recognized pattern to try. Young brown trout are often caught by the fly fisher using a pattern of nymph or buzzer close into the margins when fishing down the side of a deep shelf.

Cast the fly well upwind and allow it to drift with the natural movement of the water. Using a slow figure-of-eight retrieve, work the fly back to the bank, ready to connect with the slightest tug from the water. Brown trout will often take the fly at the last minute as it rises towards the surface. Take time when lifting the fly clear of the water and let it hang momentarily in a tantalizing way. If a barbless pattern of hook is used, smaller brown trout can be returned unharmed, as they are the future of the water. Big, old brown trout tend to be loners, and they often turn cannibal, feeding freely on a diet consisting of fry. Muddler patterns and brightly coloured lures created to resemble the smaller fish are, when fished slow and deep on a sinking line, the tactics often used to fool this fellow.

Above: *A fly in the lip of a wild brown trout.*

Right: *The peace and solitude are as much a part of the appeal as the catch.*

STILLWATER FISHING FOR
TROUT

ON THE SMALL, CLEAR STILLWATERS, both the rainbow and the brown trout may be stalked by the careful angler. Fishing in this kind of clear environment requires skill in the selection and presentation of the fly. Once spotted, a clear-water trout can be deceived into taking a fly that is placed right in its path. Great care and stealth is required in the casting of the fly to ensure that the hunted does not see the line above his head. One mistake and the trout you have spent time stalking will be gone with a flick of its powerful tail. Crouch low to the bankside vegetation and watch the path of the trout you are intent on catching. Only when you are sure, make the cast. If using a wet fly pattern, start a slow retrieve as the fly sinks towards the bottom. Watch carefully for the reaction of the fish as the fly passes its line of vision. If deceived by the pattern, he will move upon the fly and take it. If spooked, he will bolt away and others nearby will follow.

Small, clear waters usually demand a delicate approach. Here the vast majority of fishing is carried out with a floating line and long leader. Rods for this style of fishing can be as short as 2.1m (7ft) and rated for a 3–4 line. Fishing with a dry fly can provide great sport as the day draws to an end and the trout are on the surface, preoccupied with feeding. The Adams Dry Fly is a classic pattern for this style of fishing. Presented on a long, greased leader, this delicate dry fly pattern has accounted for the capture of many fine trout. When fishing during the daylight hours on a water with poor visibility, it is often better to choose a slow sinking line and incorporate the use of an attractor pattern of fly. In these conditions of water you rely on the trout to identify with the silhouette of the attractor pattern. Once the trout has seen the fly working through the water, it generally moves in for the kill.

Many small stillwaters operate a catch-and-release policy. This ensures trout are returned unharmed to the water, unless the angler wishes to take them for the table.

THE ART OF
DECEPTION

SINCE MAN BEGAN TO PURSUE the game fish of the world with the fly, he has spent countless hours crafting accurate imitations. For the experienced tyer, creating the perfect fly is the golden bridge that will place the quarry just that bit nearer. Great pride is taken in the art, and every strand of fur or web of feather is painstakingly crafted into the tyer's own unique creation. For the newcomer to fly tying, the pure joy of catching a fish on a fly that has so lovingly been crafted is a just reward.

There is a fine line between natural and imitative patterns, a line the game fish has yet to perceive. Fishing with an imitation is the key to a pleasant evening's sport. However, many of our game fish are caught on patterns intended purely to deceive. The salmon, for example, snatches at a brightly coloured fly, purely as an act of aggression. Deceiver or imitator, there are thousands of patterns to choose from.

Flies fall into two categories. Wet flies are fished under the surface of the water and imitate forms of natural insect life, moving from the lower layers of the water. There are also wet flies designed purely to deceive. Dry flies, on the other hand, represent the adult fly, which has been blown on to the surface of the water and lies trapped in the surface film.

22

SALMON FLIES

SALMON FLIES ARE OFTEN REFERRED TO AS AGGRAVATORS. This is because once in fresh water the salmon does not feed and it is said that it takes the fly purely out of aggression, with no thought of food. Many of the flies tied for salmon fishing bear a distinct resemblance to the shrimp, a species the salmon feeds on heavily when at sea. Salmon flies are tied as tubes, waddingtons, single hook or double hook.

TUBES AND WADDINGTONS

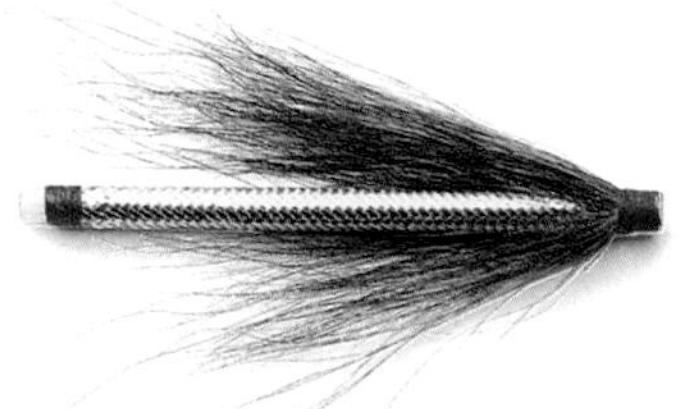

Silver Doctor

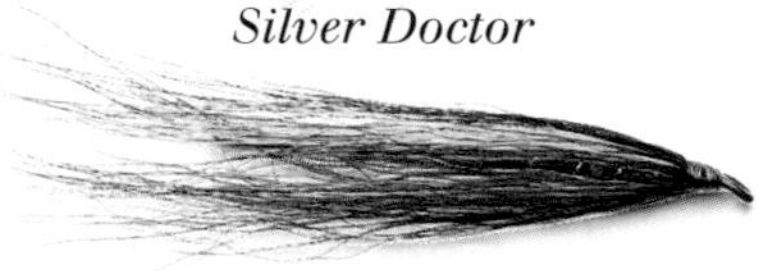

Willie Gun

Blue Charm

Stoat's Tail

Garry Dog

SINGLES

Ally's Shrimp

Rusty Rat

Silver Grey

Jock Scott

Thunder and Lightning

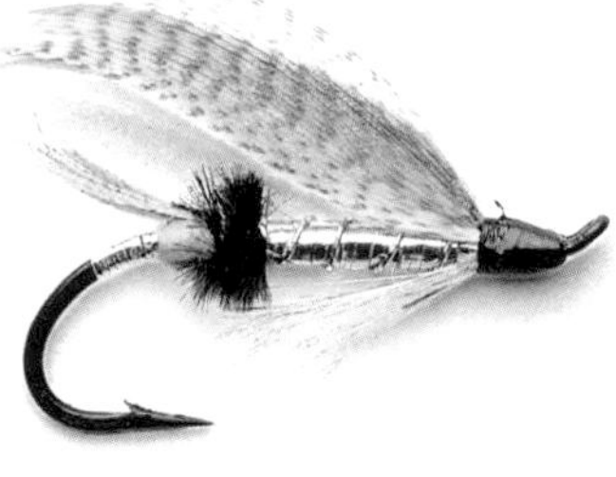

Silver Doctor

DOUBLES

Green Highlander

Black Doctor

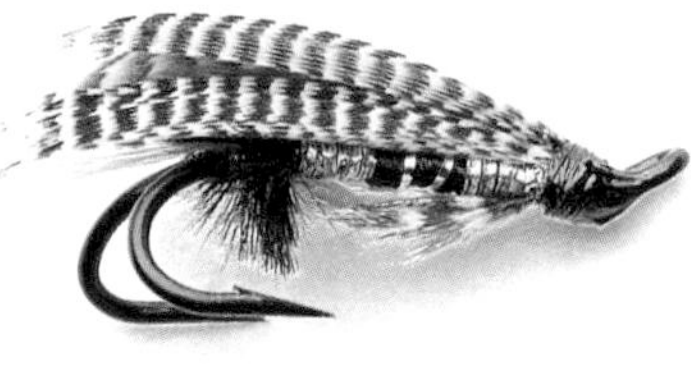

Mar Lodge

24

SEA TROUT FLIES

SUCH GRAND NAMES as Peter Ross and Mallard and Claret are two of the most well-known and widely used sea trout flies. There are many other famous patterns to choose from, all proven sea trout catchers. They are fished close to the surface of the water and should be made of light-weight materials. Sea trout flies are to be found tied on a single, treble or tandem hook.

Cardinal

Haslem   *Wickham's Fancy*   *Blue Zulu*   *Invicta*

Butcher   *Black Pennel*   *Royal Coachman*   *Blue and Black*   *Dunkeld*

Mallard and Claret   *Kingfisher Butcher*   *Woodcock and Mixed*   *Peter Ross*   *Teal Blue and Silver*

RESERVOIR FLIES

ON THE BIG RESERVOIRS where waters are deep, many anglers choose to fish with a deceiver fly. This style of "lure fishing" leads the trout to believe it is chasing a smaller fish. A deceiver fly catches the attention of the fish by its shape and movement. Lures are bright and colourful and will catch the attention of a passing fish. They can be fished at all levels of the water and are most effective in the colder months when fished slowly across the reservoir bottom.

Olive Booby Nymph

Orange Booby Nymph

Montana Nymph

Silver Minnow

Green Cactus

Consett Budgie

Gold Muddler

White Marabou

Texas Rose Muddler

Green Dog-knobbler

White Tadpole

Fritz Montana

Christmas Tree

Prince

Demoiselle

STILLWATER FLIES

Jack Frost

Chartreuse Tadpole

LIKE RESERVOIR FLIES, many stillwater flies are designed not to imitate but purely to deceive. A brightly coloured fly worked under the surface will be taken willingly by the trout. The muddler fly can provide the still-water fly fisher with some exceptional sport. Weighted versions are very effective fished down deep. If the water holds bigger fish, it is worth fast-stripping a muddler across the surface as this tends to attract the bigger species. Fished in this manner, the fly resembles the small fry on which many larger trout feed.

Christmas Tree

Bibio Muddler

Olive Damsel

Purple Damsel

Silver Invicta Muddler

Mini Gold Muddler

Whiskey Fly

Zulu Muddler

Viva

Appetiser

Cat's Whisker

Green Montana Nymph

RIVER AND STREAM DRY FLIES

WITH MANY RIVERS THAT RUN CLEAR AND PURE, the fly fisher has to look towards the more natural patterns for imitation. Smaller flies are employed to try and match the scale of the natural fly the trout may be feeding on. Both dry and wet patterns are employed depending on the conditions and the depth of the river. Dry patterns, like the Gold Ribbed Hare's Ear and the March Brown, in different sizes, are both useful additions to the fly box.

These small, clear waters are for the purist who must use good judgement in selecting the right fly to tempt the quarry successfully and who needs to be skilled in accurate casting.

Grey Duster	March Brown	Panama Dry Wing	Red Tag	Red Ant
Coachman	Black Sedge	Black Midge	Bivisible Badger	Mosquito Dry Wing
Silver Sedge	Cinnamon Sedge	White Miller	Professor Dry Wing	Gold Ribbed Hare's Ear

RIVER AND STREAM WET FLIES

IN THE FASTER-RUNNING, DEEPER WATERS, the fly fisher may need to turn to the wet fly to find success with his quarry. Old established patterns like Greenwell's Glory and the Black and Peacock Spider have served many fly fishers well. These and others are favoured for their ability to catch. A good angler, faced with a difficult water, will carry a marrow spoon so that he may examine the stomach contents of the trout. Armed with the knowledge of what the trout are feeding on, he is able to match the feed with a pattern from his box.

Partridge and Orange   *Red Spider*   *Black Gnat*   *Snipe and Purple*   *Blue Dun*

Mosquito   *Soldier Palmer*   *Coachman*   *Alder*   *Greenwell's Glory*

Olive Dun   *Tup's*   *Stonefly*   *Black and Peacock Spider*   *Black Midge*

FLY TYING

Above: *A fine selection of vintage salmon flies.*

TO BE ABLE TO FISH WELL and tie all manner of fly patterns is a great achievement. Such skills are taught by professional instructors or passed through the generations by experienced family members. To become an accomplished fly-tyer takes patience and time. It is an art that in most cases is self-developed. Patience and perseverance are the formula for success. For those starting out, fly tying doesn't have to be complicated. Don't try and emulate a difficult pattern until you have mastered the easier ones. You will enjoy your new-found skill much more taking it step-by-step in a natural progression. To begin, the minimum amount of tools and materials will suffice, until a more specialized approach has been attained.

A vice is an essential item as it provides a steady station to work from. Vices come in all shapes and sizes and will either have a clamp-on device or a solid stand fitted to the bottom. Look for a model that has a lever action jaw as this will allow you to apply the right amount of tension needed to hold the hook firmly in place. Make sure the model you purchase is the best quality you can afford and try to avoid the cheap ones in kit form. A bobbin holder with which to wind on the thread can be bought relatively cheaply, and there are several different models available. When purchasing a bobbin holder make sure it has a strong pair of grips to hold the bobbin firmly in place while still allowing the thread to be pulled from the spool. The bobbin serves two

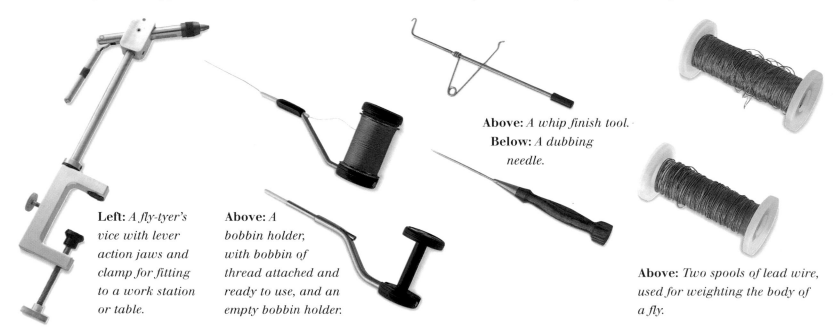

Above: *A whip finish tool.*
Below: *A dubbing needle.*

Left: *A fly-tyer's vice with lever action jaws and clamp for fitting to a work station or table.*

Above: *A bobbin holder, with bobbin of thread attached and ready to use, and an empty bobbin holder.*

Above: *Two spools of lead wire, used for weighting the body of a fly.*

purposes, first as a thread dispenser and, second, the weight of the bobbin helps to trap any materials in place when left to hang free from the partly constructed fly.

A sharp pair of scissors are essential for trimming and cutting materials. Keep them in a protective sleeve so that the blades remain clean and sharp. It is good practice to purchase a second pair that can be used for cutting wires and tinsel, to ensure that the main pair remains sharp.

For the application of fine hackles invest in a pair of hackle pliers. The jaws must be firm and close tightly and cleanly together. Check for any sharp edges – even better, buy a set that are covered with a plastic sleeve to avoid tearing the hackle. A dubbing needle is required for picking out dubbed fibres and for use as a guide needle when tying off by hand.

You will also need a selection of threads in different colours and gauges. The more popular colours – black, white and olive, are available on bobbins in fine, medium and thick gauges. Tinsels are needed for body ribbing and are available in silver and gold, in flat and oval strand and usually in fine and medium gauge. For weighting bodies on lures, a couple of different gauges of lead wire are useful. Purchased on a spool, lead wire is usually sold in fine, medium and heavy gauges. In addition, a few different coloured marker pens are invaluable for colouring lures.

Above: *The invention of the reel revolutionized fishing techniques, giving anglers a far greater fishing range.*

Right: *A selection of threads, tinsel, copper wire and silver wire.*

Below: *Fly-tyer's wax for waxing the thread.*

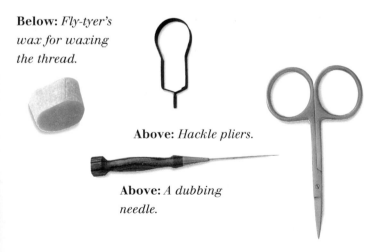

Above: *Hackle pliers.*

Above: *A dubbing needle.*

Above: *Sharp scissors.*

MATERIALS

*T*HE LIST OF MATERIALS currently in use by the modern-day fly-tyer is endless. There are thousands of natural and synthetic items to choose from. As you move from beginner to intermediate ability and your tying progresses, the need to experiment will lead you to try new materials. When purchasing, make sure all materials are of the highest quality and are bought from a reputable retailer.

For the beginner, an afternoon spent in the company of an experienced tyer is a good way of seeking advice in selecting the right materials. Choose the patterns you would like to make and buy the relevant material. If you have access to a local shoot, it is worth approaching a member, who may be able to supply you with an assortment of game-bird feathers and furs. Next time you visit the zoo, ask the keeper to save you any of the brightly coloured discarded feathers from the thousands of birds kept. The death of a pheasant on the roadside is a gift to the fly-tyer as there is a use for much of this bird's plumage at the vice. Finally, look around your home and consider using unlikely materials such as the discarded fur from a groomed pet.

Above: *A working fly-tyer's bench.*

Below: *A selection of capes have a variety of uses in the construction of flies.*

Below: *A selection of fur and hair from a deer, squirrel, hare and colourful bucktail.*

Left: *A selection of fur and feathers made to resemble partridge skin, various capes, mallards, pheasants.*

Hook Patterns

HOOKS FORM THE BASE OF MANY FLY PATTERNS and are available in various shapes, weights, sizes and wire gauges. Some are shaped to imitate the body shape of the natural insect. The size of the hook and gauge of wire help determine which pattern of fly is tied on to it. A light wire hook is ideal for a pattern of fly presented on, or near, the surface, and a heavy wire hook is perfect for fishing a fly at depth.

SALMON SINGLE – *Used for dressing a salmon fly. It has an upturned eye, which lends itself to the turle knot used to connect the fly to the leader. The knot holds the fly upright. It grips the fly from behind the eye, allowing no flexibility where the knot meets the hook.*

STREAMER HOOK – *The streamer (or lure) hook is widely used for tying fry imitations and large attractor patterns. It has a long shank and is made from heavy gauge wire, making it the most suitable choice for larger patterns of fly. It is available in barbless patterns.*

NYMPH HOOK – *This hook has a long shank that is essential for imitating the long bodies of the natural insect at larvae stage. The gauge of wire varies depending upon the depth at which the fly is to be fished. A tight coil of lead wire can be wound down the shank to give additional weight.*

MAYFLY HOOK – *Designed to imitate the mayfly in its natural state. The longer shank aids construction of the long body needed to represent this fly. Made from a medium gauge wire, it is buoyant and floats on the surface film.*

SPROAT HOOK – *Used for the production of wet fly patterns. Used for attractor, traditional and imitative patterns, it is fished below the surface. It is a down-eyed pattern made from heavy gauge wire. A popular choice for beaded flies, it can also be used for sea trout, trout and grayling flies.*

SEDGE HOOK – *Constructed from a heavy gauge of wire. It has a wide gap between the hook point and shank. It is used for dressing curved and bulky-bodied flies and is an ideal subject for adding to a lead underbody. Originally designed for tying sedge pupae imitations, it is also used for tying shrimp flies.*

GRUB HOOK – *Used in tying curved-bodied imitations fished below the surface. It is a popular choice for tying grayling bugs, when used in small sizes, and for imitating buzzer patterns. The wire is strong and heavy.*

DOWN-EYED DRY FLY HOOK – *This fine wire hook is used for constructing buoyant dry flies. It requires minimal dressing with fine materials. Most commonly used in sizes 10–18. It is suitable for use on both river and stillwater.*

UP-EYED DRY FLY HOOK – *This well-established pattern is of a fine- to medium-gauge wire and is commonly used to imitate adult natural insects. The majority of patterns tied on this hook will be of an up-wing and heavily hackled design. This makes the fly very buoyant.*

MIDGE HOOK – *Produced in very small sizes and used for the imitation of minute natural insects found on or near the surface of the water. It is of a very fine wire gauge, allowing minimal use of materials to keep it afloat. When the trout are on the surface feeding on minuscule life forms, this is the perfect pattern of hook.*

TYING ON

THE FIRST STEP IN MAKING A FLY is learning to tie the thread neatly on to the hook. Threads vary in colour and diameter (although black is the most commonly used) depending on the pattern of fly being tied, so before you begin to tie make sure you have selected the correct thread.

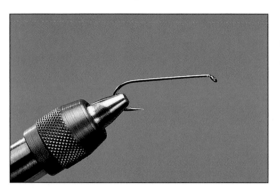

1 *Secure the hook firmly between the jaws of the vice so that the hook will not slip.*

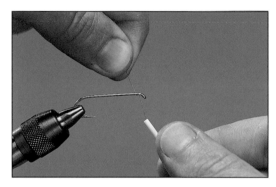

4 *Start to wind the bobbin holder up over the shank, tightly trapping the loose thread.*

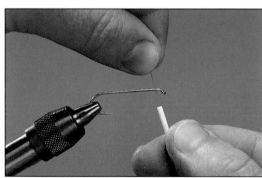

2 *Offer up the thread behind the shank of the hook and near to the eye.*

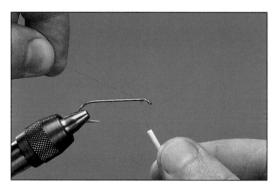

5 *Repeat this process towards the bend of the hook in neat touching turns.*

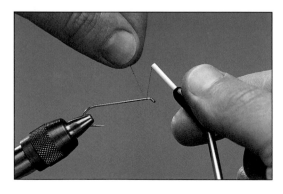

3 *Bring the bobbin forward of the hook, keeping the thread taut at all times.*

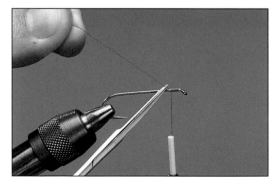

6 *Trim the trapped tail to complete tying on.*

FINISHING OFF

AT THE END OF THE PROCESS, when the dressed fly is ready to be finished, the thread should be at the eye of the hook. The sequence below shows how to make a hand whip finish. Alternatively, a whip finish tool can be used to achieve the same effect.

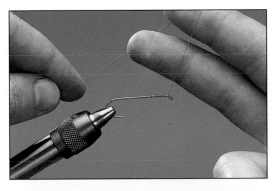

1 *With the bobbin in the left hand, wrap the thread over the forefinger and middle finger of the right hand.*

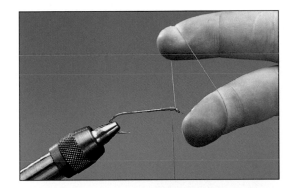

4 *Repeat this movement towards the eye of the hook. Maintain an even tension on the loop at all times.*

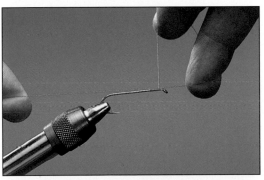

2 *Catch the thread behind the middle finger and form a loop above the hook shank, keeping the thread tight.*

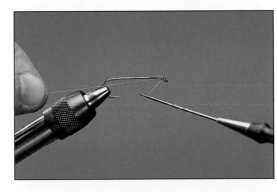

5 *Using a dubbing needle, close down the loop fully by pulling on the bobbin thread.*

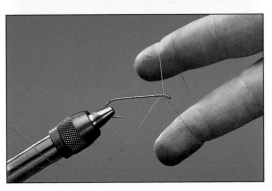

3 *Twist the fingers holding the loop around the hook shank, trapping the bobbin thread.*

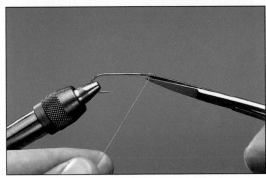

6 *Trim off the waste thread with scissors. Varnish the fly to the required finish.*

TYING A TAIL

TAILS CAN TAKE ON AN IMITATIVE OR ATTRACTOR ROLE. Materials for the imitative fly tail include golden pheasant crest or tippets, pheasant tail, hackle fibres, squirrel tail, bucktail and deer hair. For an attractor pattern, use materials such as marabou and a wide variety of flosses.

A selection of tail materials including golden pheasant crest, golden pheasant tippets, teal flank feather and squirrel tail.

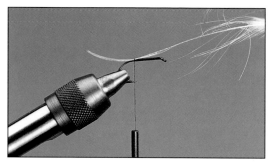

2 *Position the material on top of the shank and catch it in with a tight turn of bobbin thread. Keep the material uniform and straight.*

3 *Take the bobbin thread in neat touching turns, back towards the eye, forming enough turns to secure the material. Trim any waste.*

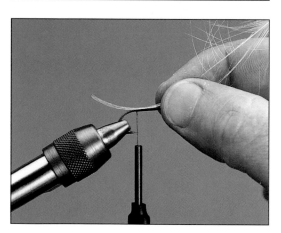

1 *Tie on a neat foundation of thread along the shank of the hook to the bend. Offer up the selected material at the bend of the hook.*

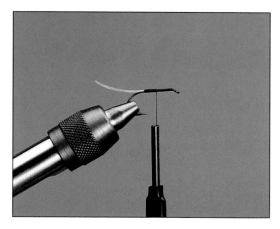

4 *The bobbin is in a position to construct the body.*

DUBBING

THERE ARE MANY DIFFERENT METHODS of forming the body of a fly. A widely practised method is to dub the body using either natural or synthetic materials. This process involves applying material fibres to the bobbin thread to form a rope. The rope is then wound around the shank of the hook, creating the body. Some materials are difficult to dub on to a plain thread. If you have difficulty, use a waxed thread instead. Pre-waxed thread is available from suppliers, or you can treat plain thread with fly-tyer's wax.

The most widely used fur for dubbing is that from a hare's mask. Its precise use depends on the area of the mask from which the hair is selected.

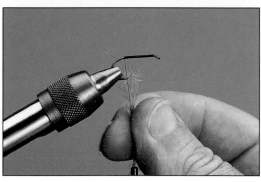

1 Prepare a foundation of neat touching turns down to the bend of the hook. Offer up a small pinch of the prepared fur to the bobbin thread.

2 Using the thumb and forefinger, roll the fur in one direction so that it binds to the thread, forming a rope.

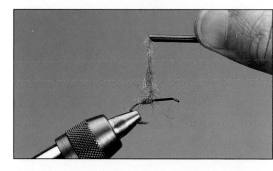

3 Carefully wind the rope up and over the hook shank, moving down towards the eye in even turns.

4 Use a dubbing needle to carefully pick out fibres between the bobbin threads to create the desired effect.

TYING A HACKLE

HACKLES IMITATE THE LEGS of the natural insect on both dry and wet fly patterns. On a dry fly pattern the hackle is used to provide buoyancy, enabling the fly to sit in the surface film of the water. The density of the hackle determines the buoyancy of the fly.

Hackles are formed using a wide range of materials, most usually feathers from a variety of genetically reared fowl. Selection of the feather used and the area of the cape it is taken from will depend upon the type of hackle required. A pair of hackle pliers is required to ensure the hackle is wound smoothly.

1 *Offer up the hackle to the head of the fly, ensuring the good side of the hackle is facing forward.*

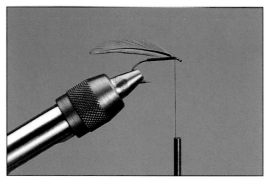

2 *Secure the hackle in place with four or five turns of thread. Check that the good side of the hackle is still facing forward.*

3 *Carefully trap the end of the hackle in the jaws of the hackle pliers and slowly begin to wind the hackle around the shank of the hook, working towards the eye.*

4 *The hackle is trapped by the bobbin thread. Trim away any waste material carefully.*

TYING WINGS

WINGS ARE USED EITHER to imitate the wings of a natural insect in its emergent or adult form or to add movement to a fly. Different material is used, depending on the required effect. The step sequence below shows you how to construct a wing using paired feathers or slips.

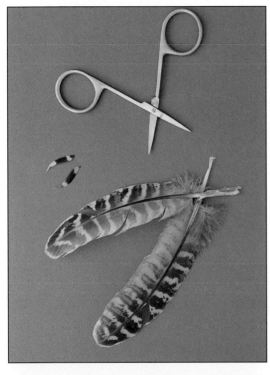

Of the many different materials used to construct the wings of a fly, feather fibre is among the most common. These slips must be selected from two matching feathers taken from each side of the fowl.

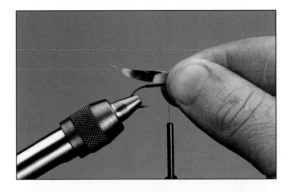

2 *The slips will naturally bond together. Offer up the slips to the head of the hook above the shank.*

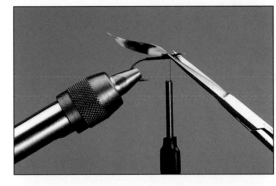

3 *Wrap the bobbin thread over the paired slips enough times to secure the wings to the hook shank. The position of the wings must remain upright. Trim any excess fibre.*

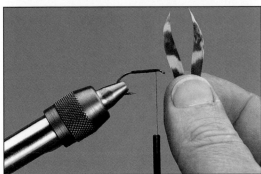

1 *Select two slips that are identical in length, width and colour variations and hold them together.*

4 *The wing is ready to receive a hackle or a whip finish.*

ADAMS DRY FLY

THE ADAMS DRY FLY is a good all-round dry fly. It is an up-wing pattern and one of the most widely used. When tied in a variety of sizes, the pattern imitates a host of different adult naturals.

MATERIALS

Hook: *Up-eyed dry fly hook. Size 10–16*
Thread: *Fine, grey*
Tail: *A mix of grizzle and red game cock hackle fibres*
Body: *Muskrat grey underbody fur*
Hackle: *Matching grizzle and red game cock hackles*
Clear varnish

1 *Lay a neat foundation thread. Tie a bunch of mixed grizzle and red game cock hackle fibres for the tail.*

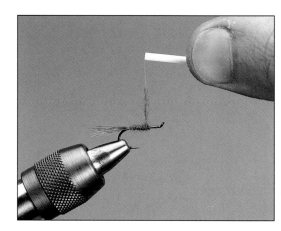

3 *Dub the body using neat, touching turns to a point halfway along the hook shank.*

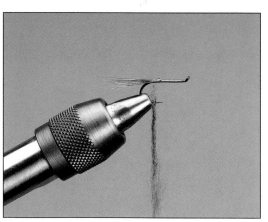

2 *Bind the tail firmly to the hook shank and trim any waste. For the body, prepare a rope of muskrat fur.*

4 *For the hackles, tie the grizzle and red game cock hackles to the front of the dubbed body, ensuring that the best sides of the hackles face the front. Trim any waste material.*

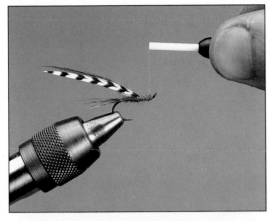

5 *Dub the front half of the body with muskrat fur to a point just short of the eye of the hook.*

8 *Trap the red game cock hackle with the bobbin thread at the same point as the grizzle hackle, and secure with a few tight turns of thread.*

6 *Wind the grizzle hackle over the front body fur towards the eye of the hook in firm, neat turns. Trap the hackle in position with the bobbin thread. Tie off and trim any waste.*

9 *Trim any waste materials, being careful not to cut the bobbin thread.*

7 *Repeat the process with the red game hackle. Keep the turns firm without breaking the hackle.*

10 *Build up a neat head of thread and whip finish. Varnish the fly's head to finish.*

SILVER INVICTA

THE SILVER INVICTA, although an old and classic wet fly pattern, has stood the test of time well. This time-honoured fly is regularly used by trout anglers who choose to fish, employing the traditional "loch-style" method, from a drifting boat. It is favoured by those pursuing salmon and sea trout when river or loch fishing.

MATERIALS

Hook: *Wet fly sproat. Size 8–14*
Thread: *Black*
Rib: *Medium silver wire*
Tail: *Golden pheasant crest*
Body: *Flat silver tinsel*
Hackle: *Red game cock*
False hackle: *Blue jay*
Wing: *Paired hen pheasant slips*
Clear varnish

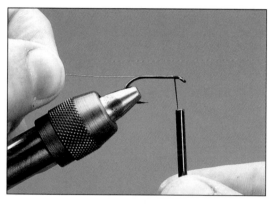

1 *Tie on the thread, then neatly tie in a length of silver wire. Take the thread in neat, touching turns down to the bend of the hook.*

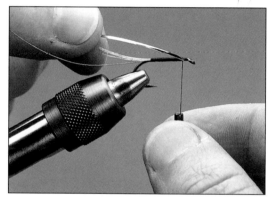

3 *Take the thread in neat, touching turns back towards the eye of the hook.*

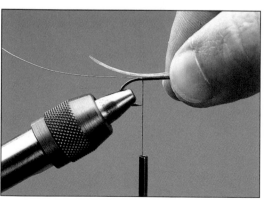

2 *For the tail, select a bunch of golden pheasant crest. Position the fibres on top of the hook, then tie in at the bend of the hook. Trim any waste material.*

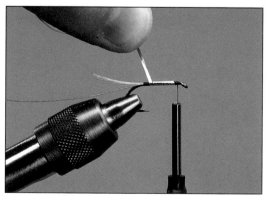

4 *To form the body, offer up a length of silver tinsel. Tie it in and wind it back to the bend of the hook in close, touching turns.*

5 *Bring the tinsel back down the hook, forming a neat and flat double layer. Tie off the tinsel at the head near the eye of the hook and trim any waste.*

6 *For the hackle, tie in a prepared red game cock hackle.*

7 *Clamp the tip of the hackle in the jaws of the hackle pliers and wind the hackle in even turns down to the bend of the hook.*

8 *Take the silver wire up and over the shank of the hook, trapping the tip of the cock hackle.*

9 *With the silver wire, rib the body in neat turns back to the eye of the hook, trapping it in place with a few firm turns of thread. Trim off any excess wire.*

10 *To construct the hackle, tie in a bunch of blue jay feather fibres so that they sit on the underside of the hook shank. Secure in place and trim any waste.*

11 *Tie in the paired wing slips, making sure that they are secure and sit upright on top of the shank.*

12 *Trim the wing and form a neat head of thread. Tie off with a whip finish and varnish the head.*

CAT'S WHISKER

THIS LURE, created by fly fisher David Train, takes its name from the white cats' whiskers that were originally used as a support for the tail in tying this pattern. The modern-day version of this productive fly is now tied with commercially available materials. The pattern is purely an attractor, with its main allure being its colour combination and mobility.

MATERIALS

Hook: *Long shank lure/streamer. Size 6–10*
Thread: *Glo-brite fluorescent yellow*
Tail: *White marabou*
Body: *Fluorescent yellow chenille*
Wing: *White marabou*
Overwing: *Six strands medium, flat silver tinsel*
Eyes: *Jungle cock*
Clear varnish

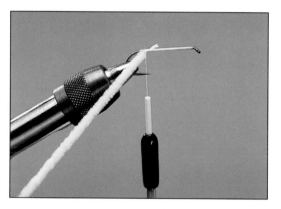

1 *Tie on, then take the thread in touching turns down to the bend of the hook. For the body, reveal the core of the chenille at one end and tie in.*

3 *Secure the marabou tail to the top of the hook shank with a few tight turns of thread.*

2 *Select a bunch of white marabou fibres and offer them up to the hook. The waste materials should be the same length as the intended body.*

4 *Wind the thread down the hook shank towards the eye of the hook, binding in the waste marabou to form an even underbody.*

5 *When you are satisfied with the length of the underbody, trim any waste marabou.*

9 *Position the wings and secure them firmly to the top of the hook shank. Trim any waste.*

6 *Take the chenille up and over the hook shank in touching turns back towards the eye of the hook.*

10 *To add to the fly's allure, tie in six strands of flat silver tinsel as an overwing. Tie in matching jungle cock eyes on both sides of the fly.*

7 *Strip the chenille to the core and tie off the thread to form a neat finish.*

11 *Trim any waste.*

8 *Select and tie in a bunch of white marabou to form the wing. This should be one and a half times the length of the tail material.*

12 *Build up a head using the thread and tie off. Varnish the head to finish.*

FUZZY BUZZER

THERE ARE MANY VARIATIONS of this buzzer, which is tied to represent the *Chironomidae*. The art to fishing this midge pattern is in the way that it is retrieved. When the trout are taking pupae before they emerge into their adult form, a slow figure-of-eight retrieve with the Fuzzy Buzzer can bring just rewards.

MATERIALS

Hook: *Curved nymph. Size 8–16*
Thread: *Black*
Rib: *Medium silver wire*
Body: *Black marabou*
Thorax: *Black marabou*
Breathers: *White antron*
Wing cases: *Pheasant tail fibre*

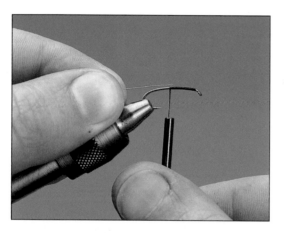

1 *Tie on. Take the thread in neat, touching turns to a point halfway along the shank of the hook. Tie in a length of silver wire for the rib.*

3 *Dub the body in neat, touching turns back down the shank, stopping short of the eye of the hook.*

2 *Wind the thread down the hook to a point just past the bend. For the body, prepare a rope of black marabou fibres.*

4 *Rib the body with the silver wire, bringing it back over the marabou in neatly spaced turns. This will give a segmented look to the body.*

5 *Tie off the rib and trim any waste wire. Tie in a length of white antron at the eye of the hook, on top of the shank. Bind with a figure-of-eight weave.*

6 *Neatly wind the thread back to the beginning of the body.*

7 *Tie in two equal length slips of pheasant tail fibre on each side of the shank. Secure. Trim any waste. Wind the thread to a point just short of the antron.*

8 *Prepare a rope of black marabou fibres for dubbing the thorax.*

9 *Dub the thorax to meet the pheasant tail slips, then back up the shank to the starting point. Fold the slips over the thorax and tie in to form the wing cases.*

10 *Secure the wing cases with a few tight turns of thread. Trim any waste pheasant tail fibre. Build up a neat head using the thread and whip finish.*

11 *Holding the two lengths of white antron tightly together with your fingers, trim to leave enough material to represent the breathing filaments.*

12 *To flare the breathing filaments, use a dubbing needle to tease out the thorax and body fibres to create a life-like effect.*

PHEASANT TAIL NYMPH

THE PHEASANT TAIL NYMPH is a popular pattern used by stillwater trout fishermen to imitate a variety of different natural insects in their nymph stage. The main materials are taken from the centre tail of the cock pheasant. For the construction of the thorax any of the following will suffice: hare's fur, seal's fur, tinsel and most synthetics.

MATERIALS
Hook: *Nymph. Size 6–14*
Thread: *Black*
Rib: *Medium copper wire*
Tail: *Cock pheasant tail centres*
Body: *Cock pheasant tail centres*
Thorax: *Hare's fur*
Thorax cover: *Cock pheasant tail centres*
Beard hackle: *Cock pheasant tail centres*
Clear varnish

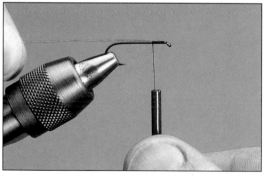

1 *Tie on. Position the copper wire rib along the side of the hook shank. Bind in place with two tight turns of thread.*

2 *For the tail, prepare a bunch of pheasant tail fibres and offer them up to the hook. Place the fibres on top of the hook.*

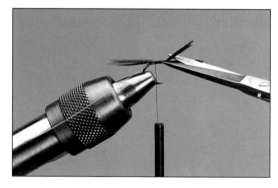

3 *In neat touching turns, take the thread down to a point just short of the hook bend. Trim any waste.*

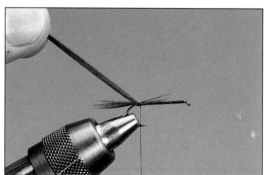

4 *For the body, prepare a slip from the centre fibres of a pheasant's tail. Select the slip from the widest part of the feather to ensure enough length for body construction.*

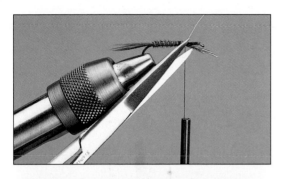

5 *Wind the bobbin thread over the waste cock hackle fibres to the end of the body. Wind the fibres down the shank. Tie off.*

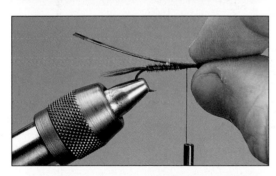

6 *Take the rib in even, open turns down the body to meet the bobbin thread. Trap the rib and trim any waste.*

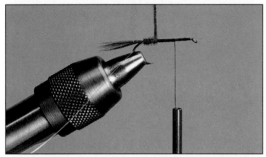

7 *Select another slip of pheasant tail centre fibres and offer them up to the hook so they sit flat on the top of the hook shank.*

8 *Tie in the pheasant tail fibres so that they start where the body material ends. Prepare a rope of hare's fur to dub the thorax.*

9 *Construct the thorax in two or three layers. Finish with the bobbin thread just short of the eye of the hook.*

10 *For the beard hackle, select another bunch of pheasant tail fibres. Tie in just behind the eye of the hook on the underside of the shank.*

11 *Trim any waste and fold the thorax cover over the hare's fur thorax. Tie in with a few tight turns of thread.*

12 *Trim and form a neat head using the thread. Pick out the hare's fur fibres with a dubbing needle to form a straggly, leggy thorax. Tie off and varnish.*

Deer Hair Fry

THIS SUCCESSFUL PATTERN can be made to imitate any number of species of small fry upon which trout avidly feed. This is a fun fly to tie and, used correctly, offers an exciting and deadly fly capable of catching the fish of a lifetime.

Deer hair is used in the construction of this pattern because of its buoyant properties. The fly is fished on the surface of the water.

MATERIALS

Hook: *Lure or streamer. Size 2–8*
Thread: *Strong kevlar or equivalent*
Tail: *White arctic fox fur*
Body: *White deer belly hair*
Eyes: *Artificial adhesive eyes*
Body colouring: *Felt pen Clear varnish*

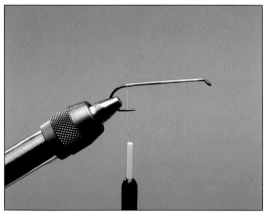

1 *Tie on the thread at the eye and wind it down to the bend of the hook in neat touching turns.*

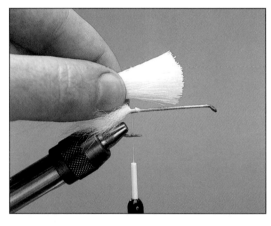

3 *For the body, select a bunch of deer hair and position it on top of the hook shank.*

2 *For the tail, tie on a bunch of fox fur at the bend of the hook with a couple of tight turns of thread to hold the material on top of the shank. Trim any waste.*

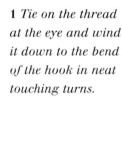

4 *Take the bobbin thread up and over the deer hair, catching it tightly on the shank at a central point.*

5 *Pull the thread tight allowing the deer hair to flare out and spin around the hook shank.*

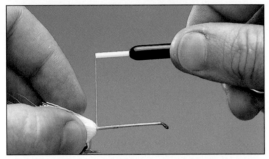

6 *Wind the thread through the flared deer hair to a point forward of the bunch. Keep the thread tight. Fold the hair back towards the tail. Secure.*

7 *Repeat, spinning bunches of deer hair until you reach a point just short of the eye of the hook. The more deer hair you spin, the more dense the body will be.*

8 *Tie off with a whip finish. Remove the hook from the vice.*

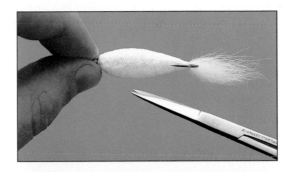

9 *Carefully clip the body into shape without catching the tail material.*

10 *Trim the threads close to the underside of the body. This will ensure a good hook hold (the hook lies vertically when the fry is being fished).*

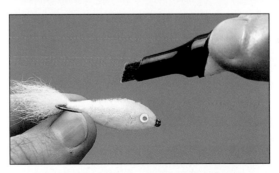

11 *Decorate the fry by applying adhesive eyes and colour using marker pens to simulate the species of fry being imitated.*

12 *Varnish the eyes and head.*

Hotspot Leaded Shrimp Fly

ALTHOUGH THIS FLY is widely used in the pursuit of trout, it also accounts for numerous catches of grayling worldwide. There are many variations of the shrimp fly. Most are constructed with the use of a leaded body in order to target fish that are feeding on or near the bottom of rivers and stillwaters. Its bug-like appearance and added colour attraction make this an irresistible deceiver.

MATERIALS
Hook: *Shrimp or caddis. Size 10–14*
Thread: *Black*
Rib: *Medium silver wire*
Feelers: *English partridge*
Back: *Pearl shellback*
Underbody: *Lead wire*
Hotspot: *Red wool*
Body: *Hare's fur*
Clear varnish

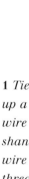

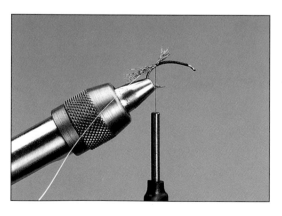

1 *Tie on, then offer up a length of rib wire to the side of the shank. Tie in the rib wire and take the thread in neat turns down to the bend of the hook.*

2 *Neatly tie in a small bunch of English partridge fibres to represent the rear feelers.*

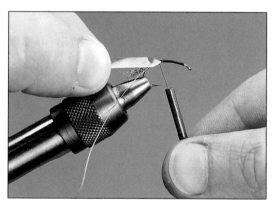

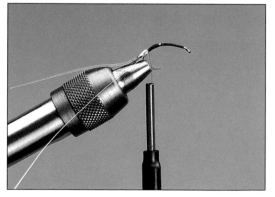

3 *Cut a strip of pearl shellback, forming a point in the material at one end to ease the tying-in process.*

4 *Tie in the shellback so that it sits in a central position to the rear, on the top of the hook shank.*

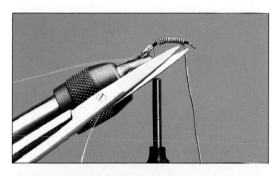

5 *Taking a length of lead wire, form the underbody by winding it down the shank towards the eye in close, neat touching turns. Trim off near the eye.*

6 *Wind the thread up and down the shank to bind and cover the lead wire. At the eye of the hook, tie in a small bunch of partridge fibres to represent the feelers.*

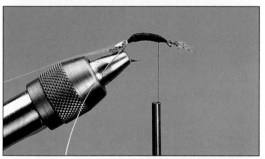

7 *For the hotspot, select a length of red wool and fold it double. Tie in across the top of the hook shank using a figure of eight loop with the thread to secure it.*

8 *Take the thread back down to the bend of the hook and prepare a rope of hare's fur, ready for dubbing the body.*

9 *Wind on the body to imitate the curved body of a shrimp and finish with the bobbin thread at a point just short of the eye of the hook.*

10 *Fold the pearl shellback down over the body to the front of the hook and catch it in with a few turns of thread.*

11 *To form the segmented body, take the silver wire up over the shellback to the eye of the hook in open turns to form a rib.*

12 *Trim any waste wire and shellback. Tie off with a whip finish and varnish. Carefully trim the wool close to the body of the shrimp to form the hotspots.*

SALMON SHRIMP FLY

WHEN AT SEA THE SALMON feeds avidly upon shrimps, but once in the realms of freshwater and on its journey to the spawning grounds, it remains in a state of fast. It is thought that the salmon still has the ability to recognize the silhouette of a shrimp and will often take this pattern in an act of pure aggression.

MATERIALS

Hook: *Salmon double. Size 4–12*
Thread: *Black*
Butt: *Flat silver tinsel*
Rib: *Medium silver wire*
Tail: *Orange bucktail*
Body: *Orange seals fur*
Hackle: *Orange cock hackle*
Underwing: *Grey squirrel tail*
Overwing: *Golden pheasant tippets*
Cheeks: *Jungle cock*
Red nail varnish

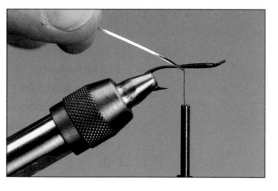

1 *Tie on the thread. Take the thread in neat touching turns to a point halfway down the hook shank. Prepare a length of flat silver tinsel and tie in.*

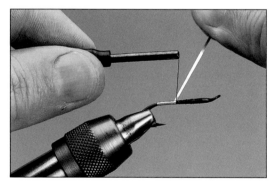

3 *Wind the tinsel back over itself to the point of tying in and catch it in with a turn of thread. Trim the waste tinsel.*

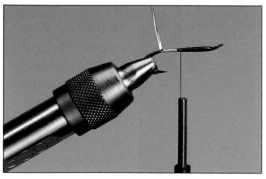

2 *Wind the silver tinsel down to the bend of the hook in neat touching turns.*

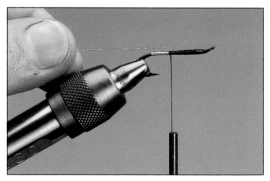

4 *Prepare a length of silver wire for the rib and offer it up to the hook. Catch in the wire with a few turns of thread back towards the bend of the hook.*

5 *Select a bunch of orange bucktail and neatly tie in on the top of the hook shank. Trim any waste bucktail.*

9 *Tie in the squirrel hair on the top of the hook projecting slightly upward. On top, tie in an overwing of golden pheasant tippets. Trim any waste.*

6 *Prepare a rope of orange seal's fur for dubbing the body.*

10 *Tie in a matching pair of jungle cock cheeks on each side of the body at a point just behind the eye of the hook. Trim any waste.*

7 *Dub the seal's fur to the hook in neat turns to form the required body length.*

11 *To tie in an orange cock hackle, trap the hackle in a pair of hackle pliers and wind on with three turns of the pliers. Tie off and trim any waste.*

8 *Rib the body with the silver wire in neat, open turns and catch in with the thread. Offer up a bunch of grey squirrel's tail hair.*

12 *Build up a neat head of thread and whip finish. Varnish the head using red nail varnish.*

TYING KNOTS

THE KNOTS BELOW ILLUSTRATE HOW TO TIE the fly to the line and to tie lines together. For beginners just starting out, practise first with string, since this is easier to handle than nylon. Knots that hold the fly should be small and neatly tied and invisible to the fish. They should have flexibility so that they move easily with the current of the water. The Grinner Knot can be tied above the eye of the hook and slid down into position. The Surgeon's Knot is quick to tie. Use it to attach droppers and to join lines. The Loop Knot is ideal when you require the fly to move easily at the end of the tippet, and the Needle Knot shows you how to tie the fly line and leader together.

GRINNER KNOT

1 *Thread the line through the eye of the hook. Form an overhand knot using the illustration as a guide.*

2 *Wrap the double thread four times.*

3 *To form a knot, pull the tag end gently and slide it down the line to the eye of the hook.*

SURGEON'S KNOT

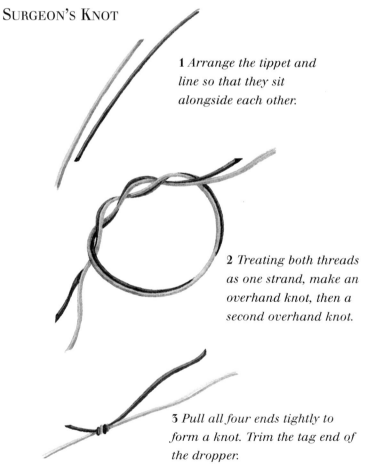

1 *Arrange the tippet and line so that they sit alongside each other.*

2 *Treating both threads as one strand, make an overhand knot, then a second overhand knot.*

3 *Pull all four ends tightly to form a knot. Trim the tag end of the dropper.*

LOOP KNOT

1 *In a length of line, make an overhand knot, leaving the knot open. Thread the line through the eye of the hook and through the knot.*

2 *Twist the ends together and thread the tag end into the knot.*

3 *Form the knot by pulling the main thread gently.*

NEEDLE KNOT

1 *Thread a sewing needle with backing and push it into the fly line. Bring the needle and thread out 1.5cm ($^1/_2$in) away, leaving a long tail end at the start.*

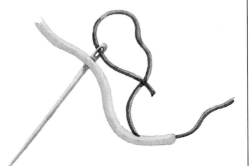

2 *Make a stitch 2.5cm (1in) long, then pass the needle through the thickness of the fly line.*

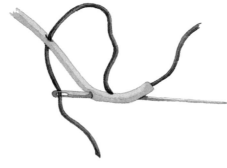

3 *Re-insert the needle into the fly line, bringing it out close to the original point of insertion.*

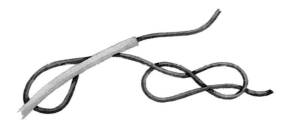

4 *Remove the needle and make a figure-of-eight knot in the thread end.*

5 *Pull the tail end of thread so that the knotted end sits close to the fly line.*

RECORDS

Type of fly	Location	Time	Month	Conditions	Results

Type of fly	Location	Time	Month	Conditions	Results

INDEX

The following pictures are reproduced with the kind permission of
Barry Ord Clarke: pp 2, 14r, 15l, 15r, 16l, 17r, 19l, 20–1 and 31tr; Fine Art
Photographic Library Ltd. & Haynes Fine Art: pp 8–9 *Fishing on a Peaceful River*
by John Brandon Smith; Martin Ford: pp 14l, 18l, 18r; and Visual Arts Library:
pp 22–3 *La pêche au saumon* by Henry Leonidas Rolfe.
key: t = top, l = left, r = right,